Published by
Princeton Architectural Press
A division of Chronicle Books LLC
70 West 36th Street
New York, NY 10018
papress.com

Printed and bound in China
27 26 25 24 4 3 2 1 First edition

Editor: Jennifer N. Thompson
Designer: Paul Wagner

Library of Congress Cataloging-in-Publication Data
Names: Rowland, John (Architect), author. | Broughton, Sarah (Architect), author.
Title: Designing Aspen : the houses of Rowland and Broughton / John Rowland and Sarah Broughton.
Description: First edition. | New York : Princeton Architectural Press, [2024] | Summary: "Sarah Broughton and John Rowland share a selection of their extraordinary body of work, revealing a holistic model of practice combining architecture and interior design, urban design, and historic preservation" —Provided by publisher.
Identifiers: LCCN 2023054930 | ISBN 9781797228723 (hardcover) | ISBN 9781797228730 (ebook)
Subjects: LCSH: Rowland+Broughton (Firm) | Architect-designed houses—Colorado—Aspen. | Aspen (Colo.)—Buildings, structures, etc.
Classification: LCC NA737.R6835 A4 2024 | DDC 720.9788/43—dc23/eng/20231215
LC record available at https://lccn.loc.gov/2023054930

CHINESE STORIES
FOUR MAJOR CONTRIBUTIONS

Silk

Edited by Li Chaodong

Illustrated by He Jiayi

Translated by Xuemeng Angela Li

RC

Books Beyond Boundaries

ROYAL COLLINS

In the 1st century BC, two major events occurred in the two great empires of the East and West, respectively.

In the Roman Republic, Julius Caesar wore a purple silk robe to the theater. Its soft texture and vibrant color sparked curiosity, admiration, and envy among the audience.

Meanwhile, in the Western Han Dynasty (206 BC–AD 25), frequent natural disasters plagued the empire. To help impoverished citizens, Emperor Yuan of Han distributed silk to those in need.

Why was silk treated so differently in the East and West? The answer lies with a peculiar little insect.

This little insect is the silkworm.

Silkworms fed with mulberry leaves are mulberry silkworms. The silk they produce is fine and long and as white as snow. Measurements show that a single cocoon spun by a mulberry silkworm can yield silk as long as 1,500 meters.

The tussah silkworm primarily feeds on oak leaves but also eats pear, apple, and other leaves. It requires little care and produces coarse, yellowish silk.

Other types of silkworms, such as amber, willow, and castor silkworms, are omnivorous. However, the silk they produce is neither as fine nor as strong as mulberry silk and yields far less.

China is where the world's mulberry silkworm industry was born. The cultivation of mulberry trees, the domestication of wild silkworms, and the utilization of silk all originated in China.

Every part of the mulberry tree is valuable. Mulberry leaves feed silkworms; its fruit, mulberries, are delicious and can be processed into medicinal ingredients. The trunk is used for making farming tools like pitchforks, its branches for weaving baskets, and the bark for papermaking.

The land nurtures its people. Its unique climate and soil gave rise to the "Divine Tree of the East"—the mulberry tree—which fostered Chinese civilization.

People feed mulberry leaves to silkworms for them to grow steadily until they spin silk and form cocoons.

How is silk obtained from cocoons?

3 Select the cocoons
4 Boil the cocoons
5 Reel the silk

1 Weave the silk

How did silk transform into luxurious fabric then?

Build the country with agriculture and sericulture as the foundation

The Han people thrived in the fertile plains and hills of the Yellow and Yangtze River basins, where they cultivated crops and mulberry trees. This combination of farming and sericulture met their basic needs for food and clothing, forming the foundation of their civilization.

With the foundation of agriculture and sericulture, men farmed while women wove, creating a traditional division of labor summed up as "men farm, women weave."

Silk from silkworms was extremely precious. Producing an ordinary silk dress required at least 3,000 grams of cocoons, or 1,500 silkworms, along with labor-intensive processes. As a result, silk became a symbol of wealth and was affordable only to high-ranking officials and the wealthy.

In the Ming (1368–1644) and Qing (1616–1911) dynasties, intricate patterns were woven into official robes to signify rank and status.

Silk products were also used as materials for writing and painting. Refined scholars loved to express creativity on silk textiles and completed silk paintings such as the famous *Along the River During the Qingming Festival*. Only individuals from wealthy and noble families were able to afford silk for creating literary and artistic works at the time.

Silk was highly sought after, and its price remained high. During some dynasties, silk was even used as currency. For instance, the Tang Dynasty (AD 618–907) designated silk as payment for private transactions.

Silk was deeply cherished by ancient people, but its production capacity was limited. To meet demand, the court established institutions like the Jiangning Imperial Weaving Bureau in Nanjing, which became famous for its silk production.

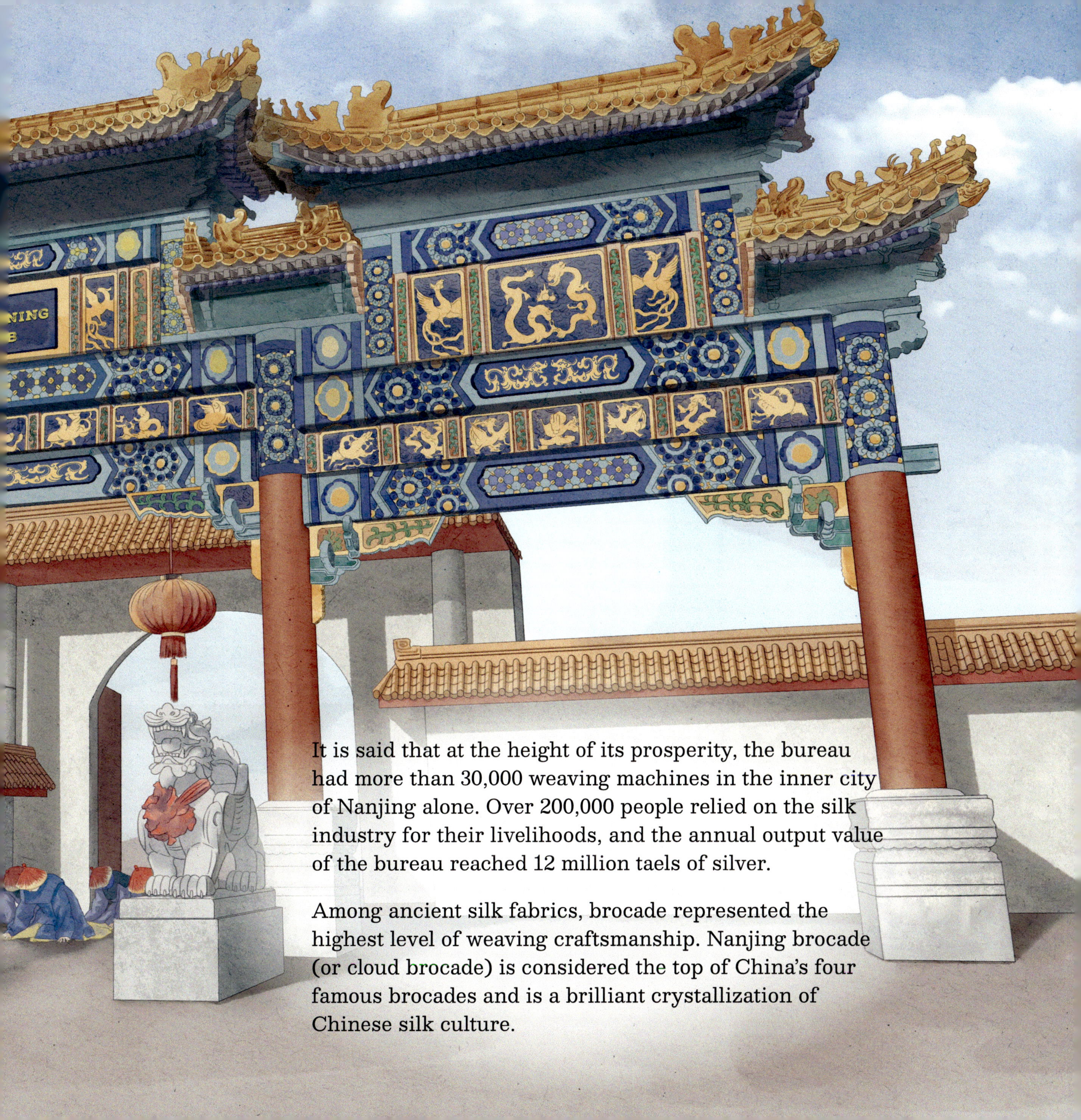

It is said that at the height of its prosperity, the bureau had more than 30,000 weaving machines in the inner city of Nanjing alone. Over 200,000 people relied on the silk industry for their livelihoods, and the annual output value of the bureau reached 12 million taels of silver.

Among ancient silk fabrics, brocade represented the highest level of weaving craftsmanship. Nanjing brocade (or cloud brocade) is considered the top of China's four famous brocades and is a brilliant crystallization of Chinese silk culture.

The Plain Gauze Robe is regarded as the pinnacle of weaving technology during the Western Han Dynasty. It is the earliest surviving garment in history, celebrated for its exceptional preservation, lightweight design, and delicate craftsmanship. These remarkable qualities are closely tied to the type of silk used and the silkworms raised during its production.

Today, domesticated silkworms are larger and produce heavier silk, making it challenging to recreate such lightweight garments. After significant effort, researchers successfully replicated a Plain Gauze Robe weighing approximately 49 grams by carefully selecting locations, planting mulberry trees, and raising silkworms under precise conditions.

Silk has held an essential place in Chinese history and has significantly influenced the development of human civilization.

The Central Plains region in China thrived in agriculture and farming, producing grains, silk, hemp, and various handicrafts. The grassland regions, on the other hand, developed a nomadic lifestyle, raising large herds of cattle and sheep and producing furs, wool, and dairy products. As early as the Qin (221–206 BC) and Han (206 BC–AD 220) dynasties, people from these regions began exchanging goods.

Exchange between different regions at the border

However, grassland inhabitants were more vulnerable to weather fluctuations. In years of insufficient rainfall, grass shortages led to food scarcity for both livestock and people. In such times, they often migrated south, sometimes resulting in conflicts over resources.

During the reign of Emperor Wu of the Han Dynasty, the northern Xiongnu continuously harassed the Central Plains region. In response, Emperor Wu sent Zhang Qian on a diplomatic mission to the West Tocharians to form an alliance against the Xiongnu. Although the attempt was not successful, Zhang Qian unexpectedly opened a trade route, connecting oases stop by stop across the desert.

Recognizing its immense value, the Han government decided to actively develop and manage this trade route, which became known as the Silk Road.

This route brought Chinese silk and sericulture to Western Asia and Europe and introduced various medicinal herbs, spices, and jewels to China.

The Sogdians were the monopolists of the trade on the overland Silk Road and established a vast commercial empire in Central Asia. The *New Book of Tang* described them as "present wherever profit exists."

The price of a piece of plain silk rose significantly after the Sogdians resold it to Rome. The lucrative profits of trade on the Silk Road attracted a continuous stream of Central Asian merchants.

Silk brought all the way from the East was light and delicate. Its color and texture were worlds apart from the linen and wool commonly worn by the Europeans at the time. As a result, silk was highly sought after by the Roman aristocracy.

The high cost of silk spurred Western Regions' kingdoms to attempt silk production. During the Tang Dynasty, one kingdom sought to marry a princess from the Central Plains, hoping to obtain silkworm farming techniques.

However, despite their efforts, they were unable to replicate Eastern silk due to their inability to grow mulberry leaves—the essential food of the silkworms.

The wealth generated by the Silk Road often led to conflicts. Stories like the Battle of Talas between Tang General Gao Xianzhi and Arab allied forces, and Guo Xin's lifelong defense of the Western Regions, highlight the struggles to protect the route.

GUO
GUO
GUO
GUO
GUO

Silk traveled across deserts and grasslands and expanded along the oceans toward the east, south, and west, giving rise to the "Maritime Silk Road."

One route started from China's southeastern coast, passing through the South China Sea and the Indian Ocean, reaching South Asia, West Asia, and even Africa and Europe.

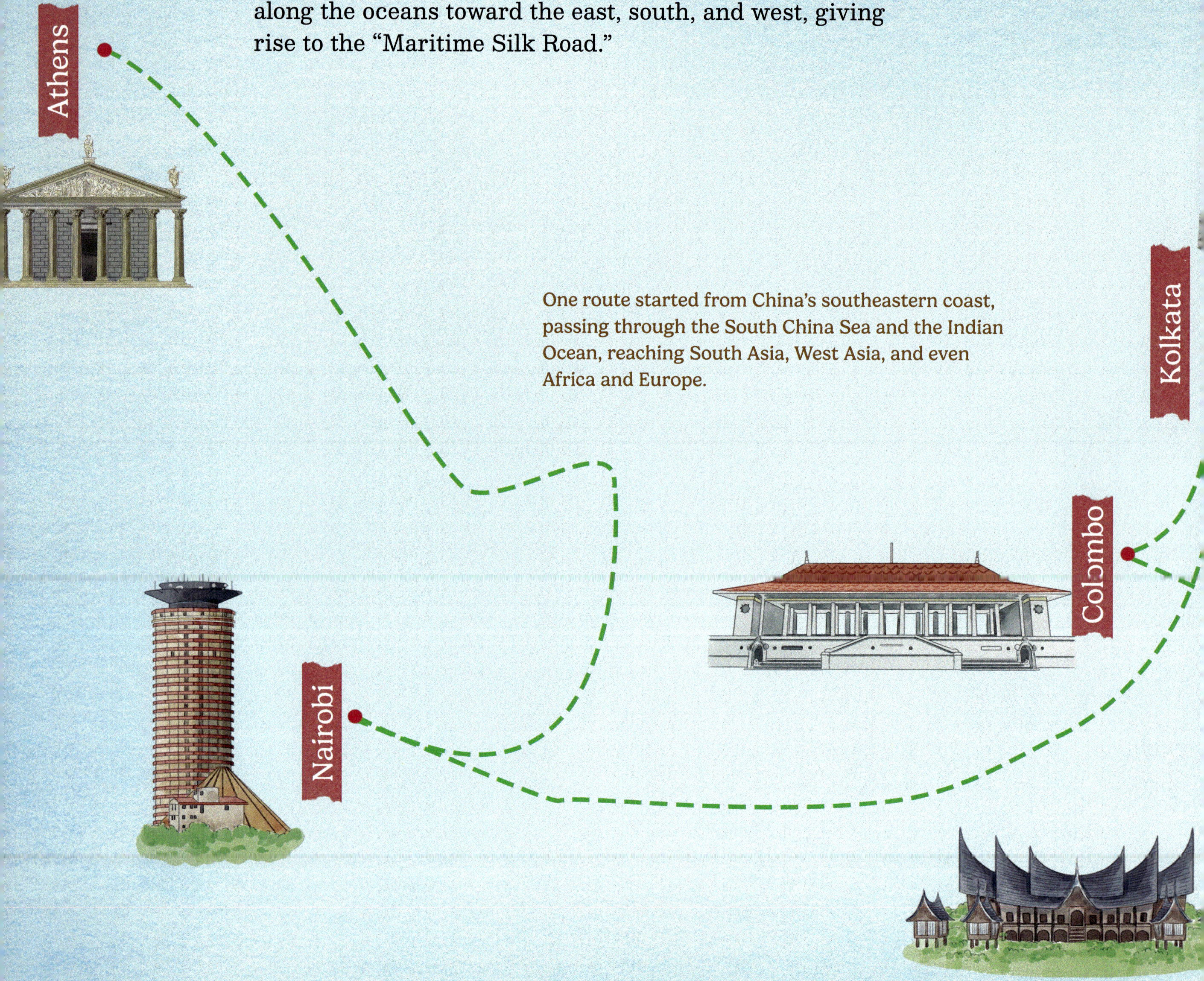

One route started from the northeastern coast of China, reaching the Korean Peninsula and the Japanese archipelago.

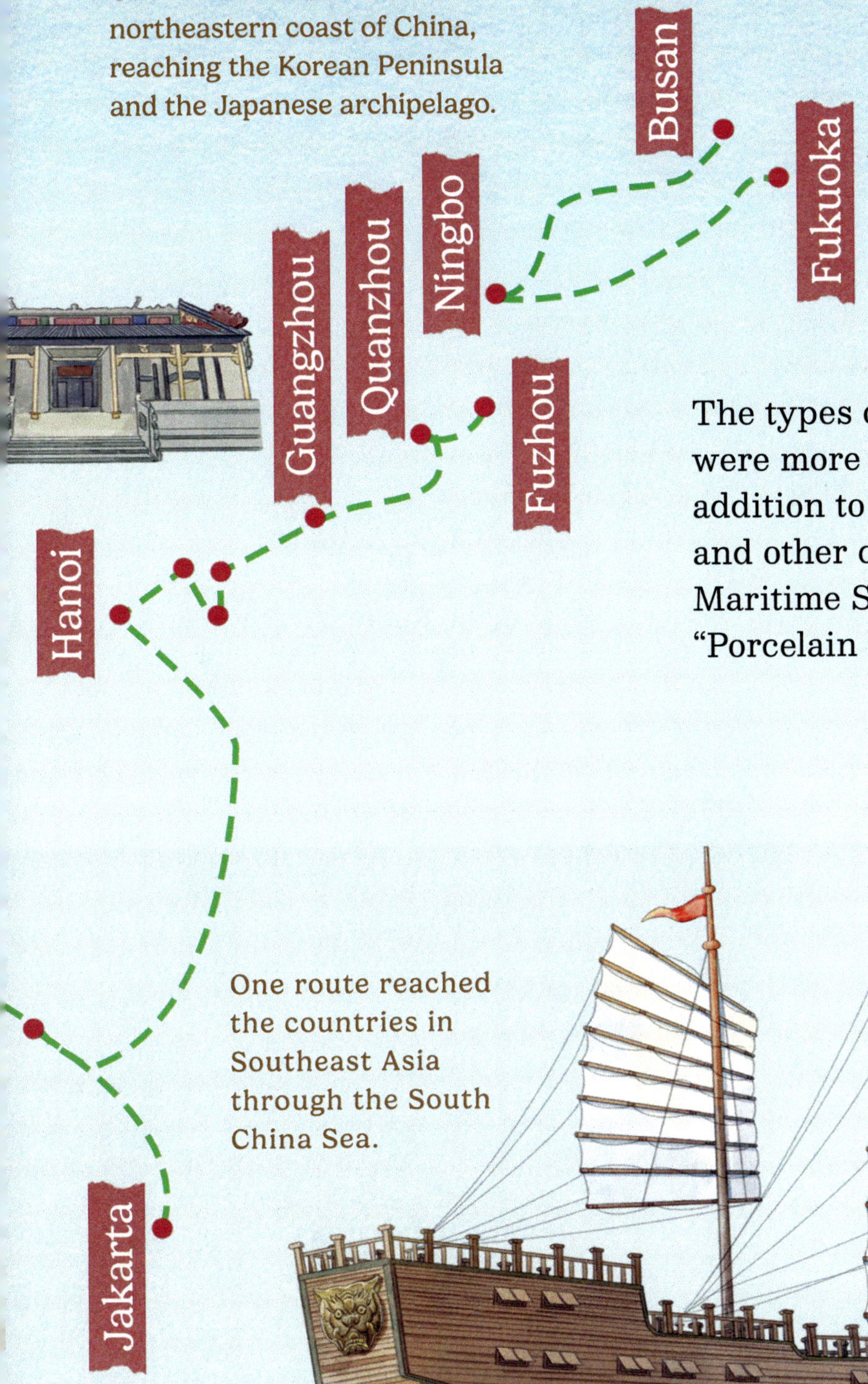

The types of goods traded along the Maritime Silk Road were more diverse compared to the overland route. In addition to silk, large quantities of porcelain, spices, tea, and other commodities were also traded. Therefore, the Maritime Silk Road is sometimes also referred to as the "Porcelain Road," "Tea Road," and "Spice Road."

One route reached the countries in Southeast Asia through the South China Sea.

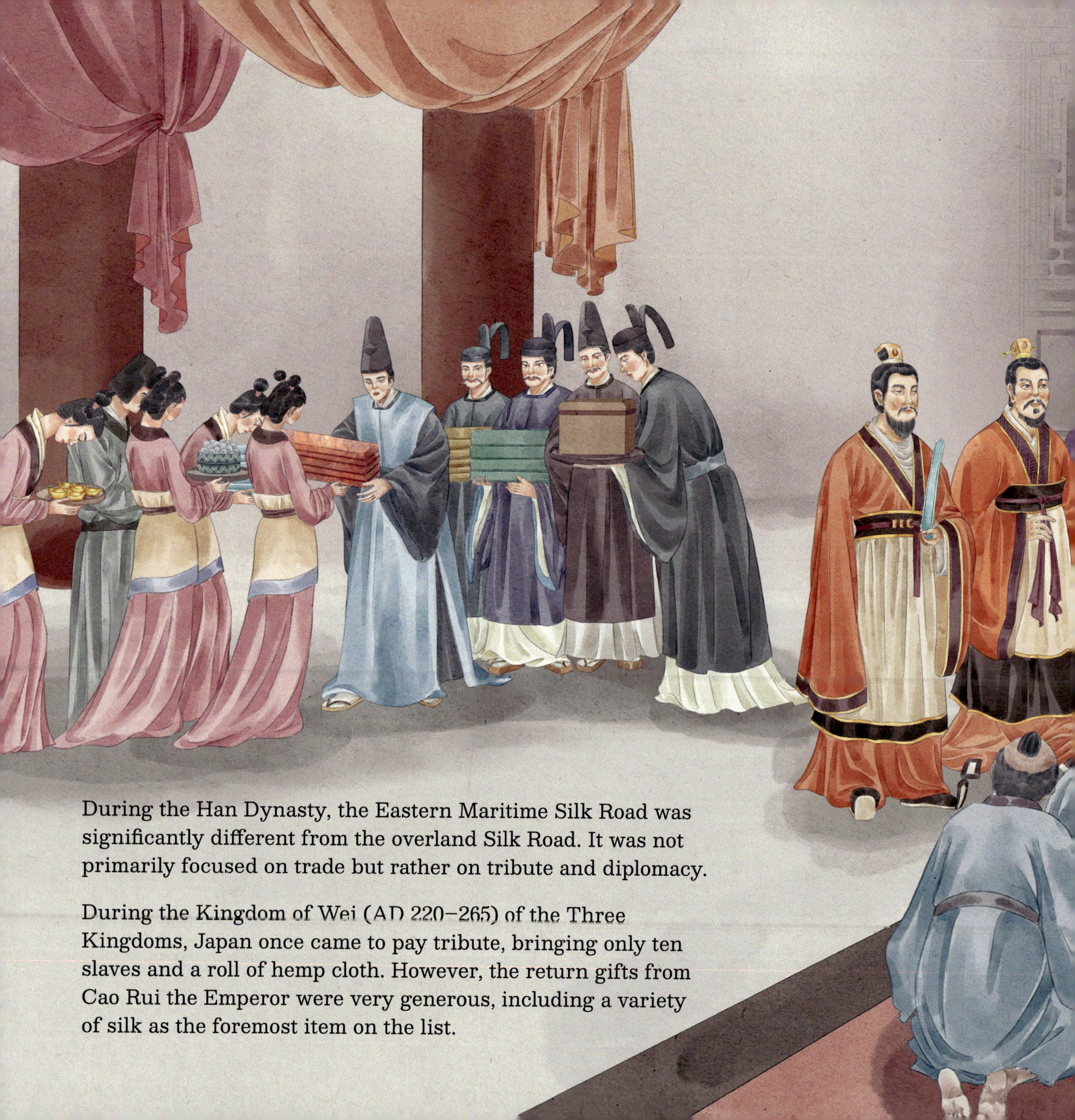

During the Han Dynasty, the Eastern Maritime Silk Road was significantly different from the overland Silk Road. It was not primarily focused on trade but rather on tribute and diplomacy.

During the Kingdom of Wei (AD 220–265) of the Three Kingdoms, Japan once came to pay tribute, bringing only ten slaves and a roll of hemp cloth. However, the return gifts from Cao Rui the Emperor were very generous, including a variety of silk as the foremost item on the list.

Due to the "Celestial Empire" ideology, China often upheld a diplomatic principle of "offering more and receiving less," providing superior gifts to tributary states. This practice made the Maritime Silk Road more politically significant than economically vital.

Through the Silk Road, Chinese civilization continuously spread to surrounding countries and regions, eventually forming the globally recognized "East Asian Cultural Sphere." China influenced the writing systems, etiquette, philosophy, architecture, and other aspects of neighboring countries.

Today, when researching the history of their own countries, scholars within the East Asian Cultural Sphere often find that many historical documents are written in Chinese characters. In studying their own architecture, they also discover that a considerable amount of designs have been influenced by ancient Chinese architecture. Likewise, when examining their traditional clothing, they sometimes find similarities with ancient Chinese attire too.

The Silk Road spread China's silk and sericulture worldwide, creating immense wealth and fostering cultural exchange.

Officials on missions, merchants eager for profit, and determined ascetic monks can all be found on the Silk Road.

Literature, science, art, and law flourished through interactions on this route, leaving a lasting impact on human civilization.

The legacy of the Silk Road goes far beyond silk. It connected nations, facilitated the rise of civilizations, and left indelible marks on history.

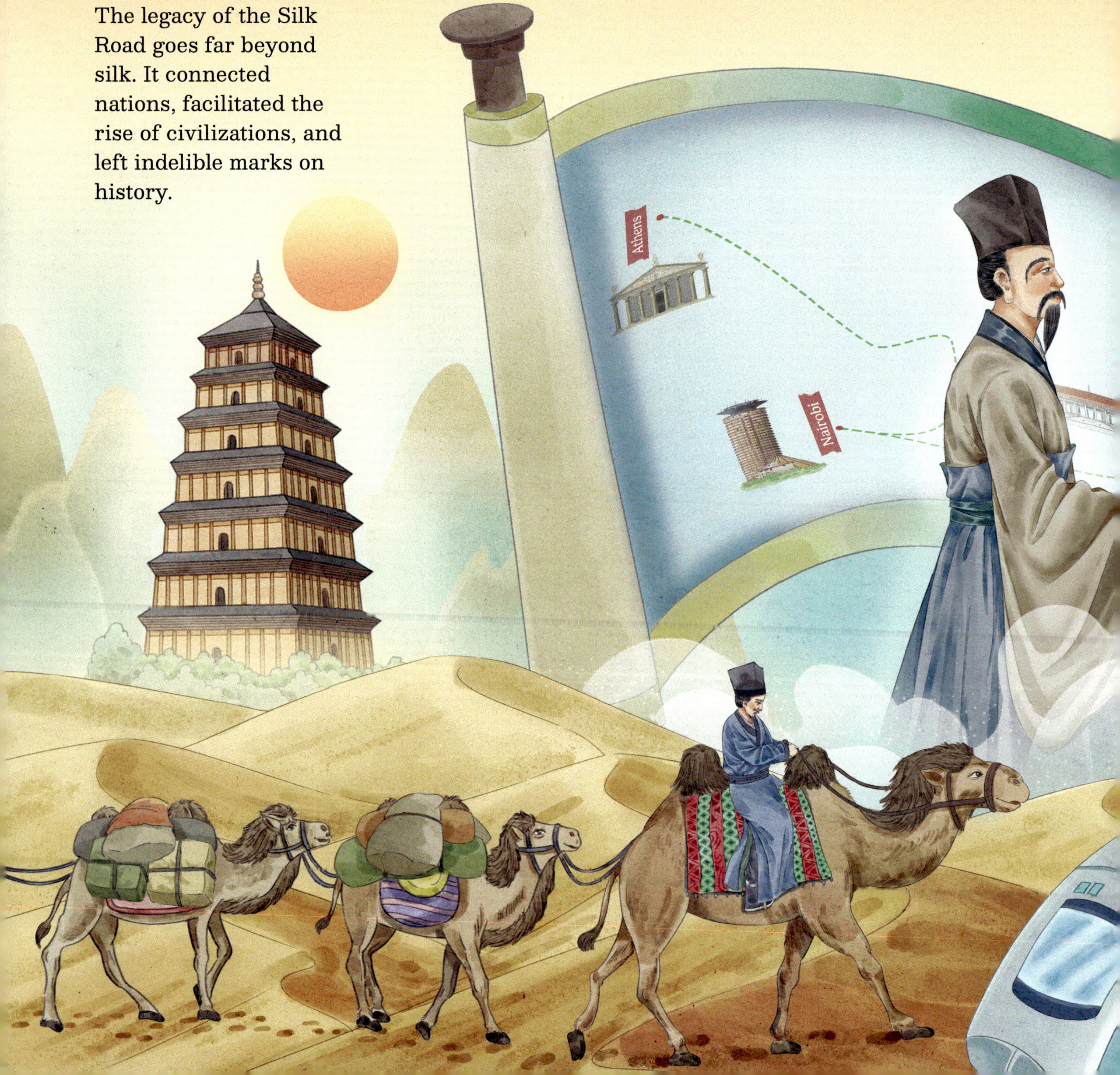

Today, China's Belt and Road Initiative rekindles this spirit, offering new opportunities for cultural exchange and global harmony. Once again, humanity embarks on a journey inspired by silk!

Chinese Stories: Four Major Contributions

Silk

Edited by Li Chaodong
Illustrated by He Jiayi
Translated by Xuemeng Angela Li

First published in 2024 by Royal Collins Publishing Group Inc.
Groupe Publication Royal Collins Inc.
550-555 boul. René-Lévesque O Montréal (Québec) H2Z1B1 Canada

10 9 8 7 6 5 4 3 2 1

ISBN: 978-1-4878-1329-1

About the Editor

LI CHAODONG, born in 1963, is a prominent figure in China's education publishing industry and a graduate of the Department of History at East China Normal University. Over his distinguished career, he has edited and published more than 50 book series. He has been honored as a "National Leading Talent in Press and Publication" and recognized as "China's Annual Publication Figure." Li currently serves as the Founding Vice President of the All-China Federation of Industry and Commerce Book Industry Chamber of Commerce, Vice President of the Fifth Council of the China Book Publishing Association, and Vice Chairman of both the Anhui and Jiangsu Publishing Associations.